Nature of Nai

Nature of Nai

Nailah S. Bolden

Nature of Nai
© 2024 Nailah S. Bolden
ISBN: 979-8-9893829-6-5

Published by Mama's Kitchen Press
Austin, TX / Los Angeles, CA
mamaskitchenpress.com

First Trade Paperback Original Edition, 2024

Manufactured in the United States of America

Cover design by Nailah S. Bolden & Emily Anne Evans
Layout design by Emily Anne Evans

I dedicate this poetry book to the Lord that I serve and the life that I have and may continue to live, as well as to the ones who gave me ideas for my free verses and imagination poems.

Contents

Foreword

Nailah. Quiet and deep. She is like the bottom of the ocean, where all of the rare natures lie. Nothing could stop her. Dealing with highschool, working on finding her peace with herself, and feeling relaxed in being alone. Letting go of all that anxiety that had taken over her life was a huge change. I am proud of her for everything she has made it through and will make it through, She is so strong.

This 16-year-old, African American teenage girl wrote a whole book, this is not even her first. She is currently writing another book called hair positivity so that people can learn to love their natural hair. I have seen her go on and off, and deal with the struggle but she is dedicated to her art 100%, whether its painting, singing, ong writing, drawing, or writing poems. This girl is dedicated to whatever she can put her mind to, if dedication was a person, I would be miss Nailah.

We thank you very much for being a support. Enjoy reading and God bless.

Diesha S. Frye, Nailah's mom

Nature of Nai

A Play of Emotions

In my heart's big play, Feelings are the stars,
They dance and spin, like planets around Mars.
Jealousy whispers softly, wearing a green hat,
But Love shines bright, and never sits flat.

Wanting to be liked, is a strong little fire,
It jumps and waves, reaching higher and higher.
But sometimes we hear, a voice that's not kind,
Telling us we're alone, but it's just in our mind.

Then along comes a Friend, with a smile so wide,
Telling us we're loved, always by our side.
He picks us up, when others let us go,
And with His love, we start to glow.

He says, "Don't worry about those who are mean,
I love you more than anything ever seen."
So let the play go on, with cheers and boos,
In the end, it's His love, that's the best news.

So no matter how you're feeling my little dove,
"let all that you do be done in Love."

Stress Storm

In the storm of whispers, I stood alone,
Rumors swirling, like seeds of stone.
Lies, like daggers, pierced my soul,
Yet still, I smiled, to keep control.
People, once close, turned away,
Hurting me with words they'd say.
But in the darkness, I held my light,
Choosing kindness, despite the fight.
I bore the burden, silent and strong,
Keeping secrets, to spare the throng.
Shielding others from my pain,
Lest worry add to the strain.
Last year was a tempest, a relentless gale,
But through it all, I did not fail.
For in the chaos, I found my grace,
A strength within, no storm could erase.

The Year of Colors

In a year of swirling shades,
I learned colors don't always stay.
Some were bright and some were dull,
Revealing truths, both harsh and full.

I plant my seeds in healthier ground,
Watched my mind and soul rebound.
Grew my faith like a tree so tall,
Learned to stand with God and my call.

The enemy came, not just to fight,
He came to dim my inner light.
But, through the dark and lonely nights,
I found strength in spiritual heights.

Friends I lost, who pulled me down,
Wanted me to wear a frown.
But I aimed for stars above,
Filled my heart with self-love.

There were times I lost my way,
Paths unclear, skies turned gray.
Spiritual battles, fierce and wild,
Tested me, God's own child.

Yet in the silence, I found a guide,
A presence where peace resides.
Now I know through every test,
I'm not alone.
I am blessed.

From Storm to Serenity

I used to be a stormy sea, with waves of worry wild,
Now I'm a tranquil lake, serene, a fearless, peaceful child.

I used to be a leaf, all lost, in winds of fear I'd sway,
Now I'm a sturdy oak, so strong, with faith I stand each day.

I used to be a night so dark, not a star within my sky,
Now I'm a morning bright and clear, where hopes and dreams fly high.

With God, there's no more fear, you see, no troubles to alarm,
In His embrace, I found my peace, my heart is now so calm.

I Am the Ocean

I'm the big, blue Ocean,
Wide and deep, with waves in motion.
Like a seesaw, I swing up and down,
Carrying boats, not letting them drown.

When the sun wakes up and shines so bright,
I sparkle and twinkle with all my might.
People like to watch me play,
But what's inside, I don't always say.

I'm the home where fishies sleep and swim,
Where some are born, and some grow dim.
My colors hide where only fish can see,
In my coral reef, where they're wild and free.

It's not easy to find this secret place,
You have to look with a soft, gentle grace.
It's where I keep all I feel and think,
Deep below, where divers sometimes sink.

So remember, I'm more than just a wave,
I'm the Ocean, strong and brave.
Inside and out, I keep on flowing,
I am the Ocean, always growing.

Spiritual Tug-of-War

In my heart's playground, a great tug-of-war,
Faith pulls me one way, to the shore I adore.
Jesus leads the team, with a cheer and a smile,
"Pull towards the stars, it's worth every mile!"

But then the world tugs, with a mighty roar,
"Come play our games, see what we have in store!"
It pulls me away, to a place that's not right,
Where I hide my true self, out of everyone's sight.

Yet, faith pulls even harder, with love so pure,
Whispering, "Be yourself, and you'll be secure."
It's a battle of choices, where I learn and grow,
In this tug-of-war, my true colors show.

So I'll hold the rope tight, with all my might,
And pull with the team that guides me to light.
In this game of life, where we laugh and we spar,
I'll be true to myself, the brightest young star.

Voyage Through Emotions

A hatchling emerges, on sands of serenity,
Innocence in her eyes, the world a new entity.
Curiosity's waves beckon her to the sea,
A vast ocean of wonder, as wide as can be.

Into the waters of joy, she dives with delight,
Each ripple a giggle, the sea sparkles bright.
Laughter bubbles up, as she twirls in the light,
The world's a playground, in the day's warm sight.

But then comes the tide of sorrow, deep and blue,
It engulfs her gently, a feeling so true.
She learns of the tears that the ocean can brew,
And the strength that emerges from a sadness she
never knew.

Anger's current grips her, fierce and wild,
A stormy sea, no longer mild.
She fights through the waves, no longer a child,
Learning to navigate emotions reviled.

Yet, in the depths, she finds the calm of love,
A tranquil below, like the sky above.
It soothes her spirit, fits like a glove,
Guiding her home, to the shore she dreams of.

With courage, she surfaces, from the deep sea of
fear,
Braving the unknown, till the stars appear.
Back to the beach, where memories are dear,
She's journeyed through emotions, every laugh
and every tear.

Hello, Brave Me!

Hello, Fear, I see you there,
But I won't let you give me a scare.
I tried to be cool, and say things just right,
To fit in the crowd, to be a pretty sight.

But then I learned, God's plan is the best,
He sends me good things, and takes care of the
rest.
His timing is perfect, like the sun's daily rise,
No need to worry, or believe any lies.

I don't need the world to tell me I'm great,
God's love is enough, and it never comes late.
Makeup can't add to what God's already done,
I'm wonderful just as I am, loved by the Holy One.

I'm a bright young girl, faithful and true,
Beautiful and smart, through and through.
Loved by my Father, who's always near,
So goodbye, Fear, I've got nothing to fear!

What They Don't See

What they don't see, the subtle shifts in her ways,
The vast change in thoughts, through nights and
days.

Guarded she stands, in a world that's so rough,
Protecting her heart from a place so tough.

Alone in her mind, where trust is so rare,
A world unkind, and people who don't care.
Through life's harsh storms, as a teen, she fights,
With only herself, in the darkest of nights.

That's what they don't see, her silent plea,
My sister's struggle, a wish to be free.

Butterfly Magic

Inspired by X'Andria Worthy

In the morning, soft and bright,
Butterfly magic takes its flight.
With pretty wings in colors bold,
It paints the sky in blue and gold.

Flying over fields so green,
It dances like a fairy queen.
Each gentle flap, a little spell,
In nature's song, it joins so well.

A bit of magic, soft and sweet,
Makes the world beneath our feet.
With every flutter, dreams take flight,
Butterfly magic, pure delight.

Rain

When clouds gather and the sky turns gray, The rain begins its gentle play. Pitter-patter on the ground, A soothing, rhythmic, lovely sound.

Drops like diamonds, pure and bright, Dance and shimmer in the light. They kiss the flowers, wash the trees, Bringing life with every breeze.

Puddles form for boots to splash, Thunder follows with a flash. The world feels fresh, the air so clean, A magic spell cast by the rain.

And when it stops, the sky is clear, A rainbow's colors soon appear. The rain, it leaves a gift so grand, A sparkling, shining, greener land.

What If

What if bunnies went to the beach,
With sand and waves within their reach?
Tiny paws on grains of gold,
Bunny tales yet to be told.

What if they wore hats so wide,
To shade their eyes from the sunny tide?
With sunglasses perched on noses,
Among the shells and ocean roses.

What if bunnies built sandcastles tall,
With turrets, towers, and a grand hall?
Digging tunnels, hopping around,
Their little kingdom on sandy ground.

What if they surfed on tiny boards,
Riding waves with cheers and chords?
Splashing in the foamy spray,
Laughing in their bunny way.

What if they napped under the sky,
With fluffy clouds drifting by?
Dreaming of fields, both near and far,
Under the glow of a twinkling star.

What if bunnies at the beach could be,
A world of fun for you and me?
A place where dreams and laughter blend,
In a beachy bunny wonderland.

Fading Echoes

Once we were inseparable, like shadows in the sun,
Laughed until the stars came out, our hearts beat
as one.
We shared our dreams and whispered fears,
Held each other through the tears.

But time has a way of changing tides,
What once was close now divides.
Words once easy now seem strained,
Connections lost, emotions drained.

Memories linger, bittersweet,
Of days when our souls would meet.
The promises we swore to keep,
Now lie dormant, lost in sleep. $\longrightarrow$

I search your eyes for what we had,
A spark, a glimmer, something glad.
But all I find is a distant gaze,
A friendship caught in twilight's haze.

We grew in different ways it seems,
Chasing different sets of dreams.
The silence between us speaks so loud,
Like a heavy, hanging cloud.

I miss the friend you used to be,
The part of you that understood me.
But now it feels like we're two ghosts,
Haunting the halls where we were close.

Sometimes I wish to turn back time,
Rewrite the chapters, fix the rhyme.
But all that's left are echoes, faint,
Of a friendship time couldn't paint.

So here's to the bond we once did cherish,
A bittersweet ode to what must perish.
Though our paths now lead apart,
You'll always hold a piece of my heart.

Whispers Of Wisdom

Throughout our lives, in many ways,
Advice comes to us every day.
A whisper here, a shout there,
Helping us with love and care.

Guardians' voices, soft and kind,
Teach us things to keep in mind.
"Be kind, be brave, always stand tall,
Respect yourself, respect them all."

Teachers at school, with lots to share,
Tell us to try and always care.
"Ask questions, learn, and never quit,
The more you know, the more you'll get."

Friends with giggles, hearts so true,
Give advice that's fun and new.
"Follow dreams, don't fear a fall,
Together, we can do it all."   ⟶

Strangers, too, with just a glance,
Share their wisdom, take a chance.
"Enjoy each moment, love with grace,
Find your rhythm, find your place."

Books and stories, old and new,
Tell us secrets, show what's true.
"Life's an adventure, not a race,
Find your purpose, find your place."

From mistakes, lessons deep,
Help us learn and help us leap.
"Embrace the hard times, don't be shy,
They make you strong, they help you fly."

Elders, with years so vast,
Share their tales from the past.
"Value time, it slips away,
Cherish each and every day."

Our own hearts, soft and still,
Guide us with a gentle will.
"Trust yourself, believe, be free,
You hold the key to what you'll be."

All these bits of wisdom weave,
A blanket of advice we receive.
In every word, in every choice,
We find our path, we find our voice.

Summer Swim

In the sunny summer heat,
There's a place that's cool and sweet,
Where we splash and dive right in,
To the pool for a summer swim.

Water sparkles, blue and bright,
Glittering in the sunlight,
Laughing loud, we jump and play,
In the pool all through the day.

Beneath the surface, dreams take flight,
In shimmering waves, hearts feel light,
We learn to trust, we learn to float,
In the pool, we're on a boat.

With each kick and splash, we find,
A bond that's growing, heart and mind,
Underwater, bubbles rise,
Sharing secrets, no disguise.

We float and drift, our worries gone,
Until the day turns into dawn,
The pool's embrace, a gentle hold,
Summer swim, where love unfolds.

So grab your towel, dive on in,
Let the summer joy begin,
In the pool, we find a way,
To cherish life, come what may.

True Love's Melodies

To be loved right, it's like a glow,
A gentle warmth that you just know.
A steady hand, a calming touch,
A feeling deep that means so much.

It's in the gaze that sees your soul,
A whispered promise to make you whole.
A trust that holds through storm and night,
A beacon shining pure and bright.

It's in the way your laughter sings,
The comfort found in simple things.
In moments shared without a word,
In dreams and hopes together stirred. $\longrightarrow$

To be loved right, it's feeling safe,
In every moment, every place.
A bond that's built on truth and care,
A love that's tender, always there.

It's in the strength when you feel weak,
A soothing voice when words can't speak.
In flaws embraced and fears released,
In every heartache, joy increased.

It's knowing that you're truly seen,
A partner in this life's routine.
A love that grows with each new day,
In countless, caring, thoughtful ways.

To be loved right, it's like a song,
A melody where you belong.
A harmony of hearts in sync,
A love that's more than just a link.

It's finding home in someone's heart,
A cherished bond that won't depart.
To be loved right, it's feeling free,
To be yourself just simply be.

Why do I...

Why do I wake each day and strive,
To conquer challenges and thrive?
Through heavy days and endless trials,
Pushing forward with unwavering smiles.

I don't vent to friends who stand near,
But to a God unseen, yet so clear.

I feel His presence, hear His voice,
In Him, my heart finds its rejoice.

Why do I apologize for things not my fault,
And why not seek others' approval's vault?

Because in God and myself, I find all I need,
His love and my strength, indeed.

In me, I've discovered my true why,
To trust in God and reach for the sky.
No need to prove my worth to the crowd,
For with God, I stand tall and proud.

In every step, in every choice I make,
With faith and love, my soul awake.

Why do I do the things I do?
Because God's love guides me through.

Starry Space

In the quiet of the night so deep,
Where stars in the heavens softly peep,
Twinkling bright, like diamonds high,
Painting dreams across the sky.

Planets dance in cosmic ballet,
Neptune blue and Mars' red display.
Jupiter's stripes, Saturn's rings so grand,
A universe vast, oh so grand!

Nebulas swirl in colors bright,
Galaxies spinning in the gentle night.
Milky Way, our cosmic lane,
Where mysteries hide, yet to explain.

So look up high, and dream with glee,
In the beauty of space, so wild and free.
From shooting stars to comets' flight,
The universe glows with endless light.

A Petal's Journey

A petal falls from lofty height,
Drifts upon the river's flight.
Joined by others, soft and light,
They journey on, a graceful sight.

In unity, they find their way,
A symbol of life's gentle sway.
Reflections dance in lake's embrace,
Unity and beauty interlace.

Surprise In My Pocket

In my jeans, I found a treasure so neat,
A crinkly bill that made my heart beat.
Five dollars, a happy surprise,
In my pocket, a big surprise.

With this money, oh what can I do?
Buy a treat or maybe two!
It's like a little gift just for me,
Finding money, so happy and free.

In my jeans, a pocket surprise,
Five dollars, what a nice surprise!
I'll save some and spend a bit,
This surprise makes my heart flip!

About the Author

I am Nailah Bolden. I am an all green girly, I love nature, and all of God's creations. I am all about art and creativity. It is beautiful to see what a caterpillar can become when it finally exits its cocoon and sees life in a new way.

mamaskitchenpress.com

Mama's Kitchen Press believes that stories affirm our humanity. It is our mission to publish stories that are personal, heartfelt, and intimate.

youthwriterscamp.com

This book was created as part of Youth Writer's Camp, a program that follows a 10-Week Social-Emotional Curriculum promoting positive mental health, educational, and economic outcomes among youth.

The aim of Youth Writer's Camp is to:
• Teach adaptive social and emotion regulation skills
• Improve effective communication skills
• Increase literacy skills through creative written expression
• Empower youth by amplifying their voices to tell their stories
• Support each youth in becoming a published writer